*365 Women's
Reflections on*
MEN

365 Women's Reflections on MEN

Edited by
Catherine M. Edmonson

A

Adams Media Corporation
Holbrook, Massachusetts

Published by Adams Media Corporation
260 Center Street, Holbrook, MA 02343

ISBN: 1-55850-642-X

Printed in Canada.

J I H G F E D C B A

Library of Congress Cataloging-in-Publication Data
365 women's reflections on men / edited by Catherine M. Edmonson.
p.   cm.
Includes bibliographical references.
ISBN 1-55850-642-X (pbk.)
1. Men—Quotations, maxims, etc. I. Edmonson, Catherine M.
PN6084.M4A14   1996
305.31—dc20   96-38368
CIP

*This book is available at quantity discounts for bulk purchases.
For information, call 1-800-872-5627 (in Massachusetts, 617-767-8100).*

Visit our home page at http://www.adamsmedia.com

Contents

I would venture to guess that Anon, who wrote so many poems without signing them, was often a woman.

—*Virginia Woolf*

Equality

$\mathcal{I}$t was we, the people; not we, the white male citizens; nor yet we, the male citizens; but we, the whole people, who formed the Union. . . . Men, their rights and nothing more; women, their rights and nothing less.

— *Susan B. Anthony*

*O*ne of the things about equality is not just that you be treated equally to a man, but that you treat yourself equally to the way you treat a man.

— *Marlo Thomas*

I'm not denyin' the women are foolish. God Almighty made 'em to match the men.

— *George Eliot (Mary Ann Evans)*

*R*emember the Ladies, and be more generous and favorable to them than your ancestors. Do not put such unlimited power into the hands of the Husbands. Remember all men would be tyrants if they could. If particular care and attention is not paid to the Ladies we are determined to foment a Rebellion, and will not hold ourselves bound by any Laws in which we have no voice, or Representation.

— *Abigail Adams*

I ask no favors for my sex. . . . All I ask of our brethren is that they will take their feet from off our necks.

— *Sarah Moore Grimké*

*O*ur struggle today is not to have a female Einstein get appointed as an assistant professor. It is for a woman schlemiel to get as quickly promoted as a male schlemiel.

— *Bella Abzug*

$\mathcal{W}$hat women want is what
men want. They want respect.

— *Marilyn Vos Savant*

$\mathcal{T}$he Golden Rule works for men as written, but for women it should go the other way around. We need to do unto ourselves as we do unto others.

— *Gloria Steinem*

[That little man in black says] woman can't have as much rights as man because Christ wasn't a woman. Where did your Christ come from? . . . From God and a woman. Man had nothing to do with him.

— *Sojourner Truth*

$\mathcal{G}$ believe in equality. Bald men should marry bald women.

— *Fiona Pitt-Kethley*

Every time we liberate a woman,
we liberate a man.

— *Margaret Mead*

$\mathcal{A}$ . . . young man put the old question, "Do you really care about all this equal rights business? Wouldn't you rather be adored?"

My answer was firm. "No, I would rather *not* be adored. It's been tried, but it just makes me nervous."

— *Caroline Bird*

*T*he freer that women become,
the freer men will be.
Because when you enslave someone —
you are enslaved.

— *Louise Nevelson*

$\mathcal{A}$merican men have had a hard struggle for their own liberty, and some of them are afraid there will not be liberty enough to go around.

— *Josephine K. Henry*

We hold these truths to be self-evident, that all men and women are created equal.

— *Elizabeth Cady Stanton*

*M*en are not able to govern themselves, and it is only when women are consulted and honored that civilization can exist.

— *"Stella" (Anonymous)*

I am not belittling the brave pioneer men, but the sunbonnet as well as the sombrero has helped to settle this glorious land of ours.

— *Edna Ferber*

$\mathcal{I}$t should be remarked that, as the principle of liberty is better understood, and more nobly interpreted, a broader protest is made in behalf of woman. As men become aware that few have had a fair chance, they are inclined to say that no women have had a fair chance.

— *(Sarah) Margaret Fuller*

$\mathcal{M}$en are very human. God made them to match the women.

— *Abigail Scott Duniway*

One distressing thing is the way men react to women who assert their equality: their ultimate weapon is to call them unfeminine. They think she is anti-male; they even whisper that she's probably a lesbian.

— *Shirley Chisholm*

The liberation of women is for women, not for men. We don't have to have anything to do with the men at all. They've taken excellent care of themselves.

— *Jill Johnston*

Power

*B*ut I have noticed this about ambitious men, or men in power — they fear even the slightest and least likely threat to it.

— *Mary Stewart*

$\mathcal{I}$ do not wish them [women] to have power over men, but over themselves.

— *Mary Wollstonecraft*

$\mathcal{I}$f men can run the world, why can't they stop wearing neckties? How intelligent is it to start the day by tying a little noose around your neck?

— *Linda Ellerbee*

$\mathcal{O}$nce, power was considered a masculine attribute. In fact, power has no sex.

— *Katherine Graham*

$\mathcal{P}$owerful men often succeed
through the help of their
wives. Powerful women only succeed
in spite of their husbands.

— *Linda Lee-Potter*

*M*en say they love independence
in a woman, but they don't
waste a second demolishing it
brick by brick.

— *Candice Bergen*

*B*eneath the veneer of courtesy and outward show of consideration universally accorded women, there is a widespread male hostility —age-old perhaps —against sharing with them any actual control.

— *Eleanor Roosevelt*

$\mathcal{P}$ower is not anything that anybody has given away in the history of the world. It's not anything antiwoman or anything else. It's just that men don't want to give up their power to another man or to a woman.

— *Nancy Pelosi*

I am more and more convinced that man is a dangerous creature and that power, whether vested in many or a few, is ever grasping, and like the grave, cries, "Give, give."

— *Abigail Adams*

*S*urely a king who loves pleasure is less dangerous than one who loves glory.

— *Nancy Mitford*

$\mathcal{I}$n a society where the rights and potential of women are constrained, no man can be truly free. He may have power, but he will not have freedom.

— *Mary Robinson*

$\mathcal{A}$ king is always a king—and a woman always a woman: his authority and her sex ever stand between them and rational converse.

— *Mary Wollstonecraft*

Oppression

*W*omen are the only oppressed group in our society that lives in intimate association with their oppressors.

— *Evelyn Cunningham*

*W*hen a man curls his lip, when he uses ridicule, when he grows angry, you have touched a raw nerve in domination.

— *Sheila Rowbotham*

$\mathscr{I}$f you got the say-so you want to keep it, whether you are right or wrong. That's why they have to keep changing the laws—so they don't unbenefit any of these big white men.

— *Ruth Shays*

*M*en will often admit other
women are oppressed
but not you.

— *Sheila Rowbotham*

So long as women are slaves, men
will be knaves.

— *Elizabeth Cady Stanton*

I cannot say that I think you very generous to the Ladies, for whilst you are proclaiming peace and good will to Men, Emancipating all Nations, you insist upon retaining an absolute power over Wives.

— *Abigail Adams*

*A*ll men seek esteem; the best by lifting themselves, which is hard to do; the rest by shoving others down, which is much easier.

— *Mary Renault*

*M*en have had every advantage of us in telling their own story. Education has been theirs in so much higher a degree; the pen has been in their hands.

— *Jane Austen*

A bully is not reasonable—he is
persuaded only by threats.

— *Marie de France*

*W*oman throughout the ages has been mistress to the law, as man has been its master.

— *Freda Adler*

$\mathcal{I}$f all men are born free, how is it
that all women are born slaves?

— *Mary Astell*

*H*e [man] has done all he could to debase and enslave her mind, and now he looks triumphantly on the ruin he has wrought, and says, the being he has thus deeply injured is his inferior.

— *Sarah Moore Grimké*

$\mathcal{Y}$ou have tampered with women,
you have struck a rock.

— *South African women's protest slogan*

*D*epictions of threatening women are common in all the arts and presumably express a real male terror of women. And no wonder! Having subjugated women in every realm of life, they naturally fear retaliation.

— *Marilyn French*

As long as men hold positions of power it is *their* beliefs that count, and they tend to see women's aggression — because it remains inexplicable in male terms — as comic, hysterical, or insane.

— *Anne Campbell*

$\mathcal{W}$omen's chains have been forged
by men, not by anatomy.

— *Estelle R. Ramey*

*N*o man can call himself liberal, or radical, or even a conservative advocate of fair play, if his work depends in any way on the unpaid or underpaid labor of women at home, or in the office.

— *Gloria Steinem*

It takes a brave man to face a brave woman, and man's fear of women's creative energy has never found expression more clear than in the old German clamor, renewed by the Nazis, of "Kinder, Kuchen, und Kirche" for women.

— *Pearl S. Buck*

$\mathcal{W}$omen are oppressed as *women*, Blacks as *Blacks*, Jews as *Jews*. But men are never oppressed as *men*.

— *Marilyn Frye*

*W*hen womanhood declares that she is no longer helpless, dislikes being penniless, and refuses to be subservient, the men become indignant and inarticulate, and find themselves caught in a contradictory position.

— *Rebecca West*

*P*rotectiveness has often muffled
the sound of doors closing
against women.

— *Betty Friedan*

*M*en's favorite method of arguing
against women is to deny
their statements of fact.

— *Christabel Pankhurst*

*M*an inflicts injury upon woman, unspeakable injury in placing her intellectual and moral nature in the background, and woman injures herself by submitting to be regarded only as a female.

— *Abby H. Price*

$\mathcal{I}$n a world where "a man's word is his honor," and where female human beings have been both silenced and dishonored for millennia, the word of woman seems a fragile thing.

— *Robin Morgan*

Careers

*D*ear, never forget one little point:
It's my business. You just
work here.

— *Elizabeth Arden (to her husband)*

*B*usiness was his aversion;
pleasure was his
business.

— *Maria Edgeworth*

The test for whether or not you can hold a job should not be the arrangement of your chromosomes.

— *Bella Abzug*

$\mathcal{W}$hen men reach their sixties and
retire, they go to pieces.
Women go right on cooking.

— *Gail Sheehy*

he only jobs for which no man is qualified are human incubators and wet nurse. Likewise, the only job for which no woman is or can be qualified is sperm donor.

— *Wilma Scott Heide*

*B*ut oh, what a woman I should be
if an able young man would
consecrate his life to me as secretaries
and technicians do to their men
employers.

— *Mabel Ulrich*

$\mathcal{I}$f a woman is sent to the Middle East . . . will she be able to cover stories there as well as a man? Yes. They may think she's a whore, but often they will talk to her more openly than to a male reporter.

— *Linda Ellerbee*

I could have succeeded much easier
  in my career had I been a man.

— *Henrietta Green*

Money

If all the rich men in the world
divided up their money
amongst themselves, there wouldn't
be enough to go round.

— *Christina Stead*

I was once so poor I didn't know where my next husband was coming from.

— *Mae West*

Anger makes dull men witty, but it keeps them poor.

— *Queen Elizabeth I*

$\mathcal{I}$t is a truth universally acknowledged, that a single man in possession of a good fortune, must be in want of a wife.

— *Jane Austen*

A man who isn't generous with
his money isn't generous
with his love and affection.

— *Georgette Mosbacher*

$\mathcal{N}$ot knowing what's going on with money in marriage is about as smart as a man expecting his wife to do all the discipline of the children and being surprised one day when one of them goes up on a drug rap.

— *Helen Gurley Brown*

A fool and his money are soon married.

— *Carolyn Wells*

$\mathcal{I}$ don't need an overpowering, powerful, rich man to feel secure. I'd much rather have a man who is there for me, who really loves me, who is growing, who is real.

— *Bianca Jagger*

$\mathcal{I}$ think women are just as moved by appearance [as men are], but they are willing to accept a situation where the man is less attractive because of the "who earns the bread" situation.

— *Madonna*

$\mathcal{I}$ never want to say to a man, "I saw this cute suit, can I have a thousand dollars?"

— *Joan Ganz Cooney*

$\mathcal{N}$ow that he was rich he was not thought ignorant any more, but simply eccentric.

— *Mavis Gallant*

Love

The more you love someone the more he wants from you and the less you have to give since you've already given him your love.

— *Nikki Giovanni*

$\mathcal{H}$im that I love, I wish to be
free — even from me.

— *Anne Morrow Lindbergh*

*B*oyfriends weren't friends at all;
they were prizes, escorts,
symbols of achievement, fascinating
strangers, the Other.

— *Susan Allen Toth*

$\mathscr{W}$e had a lot in common. I loved
him and he loved him.

— *Shelley Winters*

$\mathcal{N}$o one knows how it is that
with one glance a boy can break through
into a girl's heart.

— *Nancy Thayer*

*B*revity may be the soul of wit, but not when someone's saying "I love you." When someone's saying "I love you," he always ought to give a lot of details: Like, why does he love you? And, how much does he love you? And, when and where did he first begin to love you? Favorable comparisons with all the other women he ever loved are also welcome. And even though he insists it would take forever to count the ways in which he loves you, let him start counting.

— *Judith Viorst*

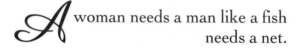

woman needs a man like a fish needs a net.

— *Cynthia Heimel*

$\mathcal{A}$merican men say "I love you" as part of the conversation.

— *Liv Ullman*

A man never knows how to say goodbye; a woman never knows when to say it.

— *Helen Rowland*

*W*hatever our souls are made of,
his and mine are the same.

— *Emily Brontë*

Of you never want to see a man again, say, "I love you. I want to marry you. I want to have children"— they leave skid marks.

— *Rita Rudner*

*B*e fond of the man who jests at his scars, if you like, but never believe he is being on the level with you.

— *Pamela Hansford Johnson*

*M*an reaches the highest point of
lovableness at 12 to 17 — to
get it back, in a second flowering,
at the age of 70 to 90.

— *Isak Dinesen*

$\mathcal{W}$oman's life must be wrapped up
in a man, and the cleverest
woman on earth is the biggest fool
with a man.

— *Dorothy Parker*

$\mathcal{T}$here are men I could spend
eternity with. But not
this life.

— *Kathleen Norris*

*A*ll men are not slimy warthogs.
Some men are silly giraffes,
some woebegone puppies, some insecure
frogs. But if one is not careful, those
slimy warthogs can ruin it for
all the others.

— *Cynthia Heimel*

A fox is a wolf who sends flowers.

— *Ruth Weston*

If a man prepares dinner for you and the salad contains three or more types of lettuce, he is serious.

— *Rita Rudner*

There are so many kinds of awful men—

One can't avoid them all. She often said

She'd never make the same mistake again:

She always made a new mistake instead.

— *Wendy Cope*

Loving an old bachelor is always a no-win situation, and you come to terms with that early on, or you go away.

— *Jean Harris*

*L*ove, a child, is ever crying,

Please him and he straight is flying,

Give him, he the more is craving,

Never satisfied with having.

— *Lady Mary Wroth*

Some men break your heart in two,

Some men fawn and flatter,

Some men never look at you,

And that cleans up the matter.

— *Dorothy Parker*

*I*f you're dating a man who you think might be "Mr. Right," if he a) got older, b) got a new job, or c) visited a psychiatrist, you are in for a nasty surprise. The cocoon-to-butterfly theory only works on cocoons and butterflies.

— *Rita Rudner*

*T*he man she had was kind and clean

And well enough for every day,

But oh, dear friends, you should have seen

The one that got away!

— *Dorothy Parker*

A romantic man often feels more uplifted with two women than with one: his love seems to hit the ideal mark somewhere between two different faces.

— *Elizabeth Bowen*

$\mathcal{M}$an is to be held only by the *slightest* chains; with the idea that he can break them at pleasure, he submits to them in sport.

— *Maria Edgeworth*

One of my theories is that men love
with their eyes; women love with
their ears.

— *Zsa Zsa Gabor*

$\mathcal{I}$f I had never met him I would
have dreamed him into being.

— *Anzia Yezierska*

A man when he is making up to anybody can be cordial and gallant and full of little attentions and altogether charming. But when a man is really in love he can't help looking like a sheep.

— *Agatha Christie*

I love you no matter what you do,
but do you have to do so
much of it?

— *Jean Illsley Clarke*

$\mathcal{I}$f somebody makes me laugh, I'm
his slave for life.

— *Bette Midler*

Love is like playing checkers.
You have to know which
man to move.

— *Jackie Mabley*

*M*en are so romantic, don't you think? They look for a perfect partner when what they should be looking for is perfect love.

— *Fay Weldon*

*C*all no man foe, but never love
a stranger.

— *Stella Benson*

What I have always loved most in men is imperfection. I get moved by the wrinkles on the throat of a man. It makes me love him more. I think it is sad that more women don't take the chance that maybe men will be moved by seeing the chin a little less firm than it used to be, that a man will be *more* in love with his wife because he remembers who she was and sees who she is and thinks, God, isn't that lovely that this happened to her. And be moved by life telling its story there.

— *Liv Ullman*

By the time you swear you're his,

Shivering and sighing,

And he vows his passion is

Infinite, undying—

Lady, make a note of this:

One of you is lying.

— *Dorothy Parker*

*T*he one certain way for a woman
to hold a man is to leave him
for religion.

— *Muriel Spark*

$\mathcal{P}$lain women know more about
men than beautiful ones do.

— *Katharine Hepburn*

When a man of forty falls in love
with a girl of twenty, it isn't
her youth he is seeking but his own.

— *Lenore Coffee*

No matter how hard a man may labor, some woman is always in the background of his mind. She is the one reward of virtue.

— *Gertrude Franklin Atherton*

Sometimes I wonder if men and women really suit each other. Perhaps they should live next door and just visit now and then.

— *Katharine Hepburn*

$\mathcal{M}$y true friends have always
given me that supreme
proof of devotion, a spontaneous
aversion for the man I loved.

— *Colette*

*P*ersonally, I think if a woman hasn't met the right man by the time she's 24, she may be lucky.

— *Deborah Kerr*

$\mathcal{W}$hat is most beautiful in virile men is something feminine; what is most beautiful in feminine women is something masculine.

— *Susan Sontag*

I require only three things of a man. He must be handsome, ruthless, and stupid.

— *Dorothy Parker*

A woman has got to love a bad man once or twice in her life, to be thankful for a good one.

— *Marjorie Kinnan Rawlings*

*A*merica's best buy for a nickel is
a telephone call to the
right man.

— *Ilka Chase*

$\mathcal{I}$ never liked the men I loved, and I
never loved the men I liked.

— *Fanny Brice*

Sex

$\mathcal{A}$ man in the house is worth two
in the street.

— *Mae West*

$\mathcal{T}$he worship of muscular male
forms is a weakness of men
and not of women.

— *Elizabeth Gould Davis*

_T_he average man is more interested in a woman who is interested in him than he is in a woman with beautiful legs.

— *Marlene Dietrich*

*M*en reach their sexual peak at eighteen. Women reach theirs at thirty-five. Do you get the feeling that God is playing a practical joke?

— *Rita Rudner*

I had the feeling that Pandora's box contained the mysteries of woman's sensuality, so different from man's and for which man's language was inadequate. The language of sex had yet to be invented.

— *Anaïs Nin*

*W*omen want mediocre men, and men are working hard to become as mediocre as possible.

— *Margaret Mead*

$\mathcal{E}$asy is an adjective used to describe
a woman who has the sexual
morals of a man.

— *Nancy Linn-Desmond*

$\mathscr{I}$t's not the men in my life, it's the
life in my men.

— *Mae West*

*W*hy are women . . . so much
more interesting to men
than men are to women?

— *Virginia Woolf*

There are some men who possess a quality which goes way beyond romantic or even sexual appeal, a quality which literally enslaves. It has very little to do with looks and nothing at all to do with youth, because there are some quite mature and unathletic specimens who have it. It's an expression in the eyes, or an aura of being in control, and responsible, or something easy and powerful in the stance, or who knows.

— *Lucille Kallen*

*B*oys don't make passes at female
smartasses.

— *Letty Cottin Pogrebin*

*L*esbianism is too near the bone
for many women, and too
disorientating to the arrogance
of most men.

— *Charlotte Wolff*

$\mathcal{M}$en are creatures with two legs
and eight hands.

— *Jayne Mansfield*

If boys are better, why should a male choose to love an inferior female? If a penis is so great, two penises should be even greater.

— *Letty Cottin Pogrebin*

In answer to "Inside every thin woman there's a fat woman trying to get out," I always think it's "Outside every thin woman there's a fat man trying to get in."

— *Katharine Whitehorn*

*W*oman's degradation is in man's idea of his sexual rights. Our religion, laws, customs, are all founded on the belief that woman was made for man. Come what will, my whole soul rejoices in the truth that I have uttered.

— *Elizabeth Cady Stanton*

$\mathcal{O}$nce you know what women are
like, men get kind of boring.
I'm not trying to put them down, I mean
I like them sometimes as people, but
sexually they're dull.

— *Rita Mae Brown*

$\mathcal{W}$hen women go wrong, men
go right after them.

— *Mae West*

*I*t is possible that blondes also
prefer gentlemen.

— *Mamie Van Doren*

$\mathcal{S}$ometimes I think if there was a third sex men wouldn't get so much as a glance from me.

— *Amanda Vail*

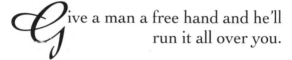

$\mathscr{G}$ive a man a free hand and he'll
run it all over you.

— *Mae West*

$\mathcal{B}$loody men are like bloody
buses—

You wait for about a year

And as soon as one approaches your stop

Two or three others appear.

— *Wendy Cope*

*I*t is easier to keep half a dozen
lovers guessing than to keep
one lover after he has stopped guessing.

— *Helen Rowland*

$\mathcal{I}$t's all right for a perfect stranger
to kiss your hand as long as
he's perfect.

— *Mae West*

$\mathcal{T}$here was nothing more fun than
a man.

— *Dorothy Parker*

*G*entlemen always seem to
remember blondes.

— *Anita Loos*

*W*omen complain about sex more
often than men. Their gripes
fall into two major categories:
1. Not enough. 2. Too much.

— *Ann Landers*

$\mathcal{M}$en seldom make passes
At girls who wear glasses.

— *Dorothy Parker*

The man experiences the highest unfolding of his creative powers not through asceticism, but through sexual happiness.

— *Mathilda von Kemnitz*

A man's kiss is his signature.

— *Mae West*

*I*t serves me right for putting all my
eggs in one bastard.

— *Dorothy Parker*

$\mathcal{M}$en and women, women and men. It will never work.

— *Erica Jong*

$\mathcal{Y}$ou can seduce a man
without taking
anything off, without even
touching him.

— *Rae Dawn Chong*

*H*e is every other inch a
gentleman.

— *Rebecca West*

$\mathcal{I}$ go for two kinds of men. The kind
with muscles, and the kind
without.

— *Mae West*

A girl can wait for the right man to come along, but in the meantime, that still doesn't mean she can't have a wonderful time with all the wrong ones.

— *Cher*

$\mathcal{I}$ always did like a man in uniform.
And that one fits you grand.
Why don't you come up sometime
and see me?

— *Mae West*

Marriage

$\mathcal{I}$ never married because there was no need. I have three pets at home which answer the same purpose as a husband. I have a dog which growls every morning, a parrot which swears all afternoon, and a cat that comes home late at night.

— *Marie Corelli*

$\mathcal{T}$he trouble with some women is that they get all excited about nothing—and then marry him.

— *Cher*

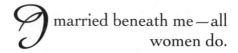

I married beneath me — all
women do.

— *Nancy Astor*

I have yet to hear a man ask for advice on how to combine marriage and a career.

— *Gloria Steinem*

They err, who say that husbands
can't be lovers.

— *Anne Finch*

*A*fter a few years of marriage a
man can look right at a
woman without seeing her and a
woman can see right through a man
without looking at him.

— *Helen Rowland*

$\mathcal{A}$ny intelligent woman who reads the marriage contract, and then goes into it, deserves all the consequences.

— *Isadora Duncan*

*W*henever you want to marry
someone, go have lunch
with his ex-wife.

— *Shelley Winters*

A woman fit to be a man's wife is
too good to be his servant.

— *Dorothy Leigh*

*N*ot all women give most of their
waking thoughts to pleasing
men. Some are married.

— *Emma Lee*

I suppose when they reach a certain age some men are afraid to grow up. It seems the older the men get, the younger their new wives get.

— *Elizabeth Taylor*

I wanted to sleep with him and I didn't know how to do it without getting married. I talked to everybody, my priest, my doctor, and they all said, "Do it. Get married." Now I could punch them in the nose.

— *Joan Hackett*

*W*hen you see what some girls
marry, you realize how they
must hate to work for a living.

— *Helen Rowland*

I have no wish for a second husband. I had enough of the first. I like to have my own way— to lie down mistress, and get up master.

— *Susanna Moodie*

*W*hat ever happened to the kind of love leech that lived in his car and dropped by once a month to throw up and use you for your shower? Now all these pigs want is a *commitment*.

— *Judy Tenuta*

*S*ome of us are becoming the men we
wanted to marry.

— *Gloria Steinem*

$\mathcal{M}$en often marry their mothers.

— *Edna Ferber*

When a man seduces a woman, it should, I think, be termed a *left-handed* marriage.

— *Mary Wollstonecraft*

I never hated a man enough to give
him his diamonds back.

— *Zsa Zsa Gabor*

The *divine right* of husbands, like the divine right of kings, may, it is hoped, in this enlightened age, be contested without danger.

— *Mary Wollstonecraft*

On the whole, I haven't found men
unduly loath to say, "I love you."
The real trick is to get them to say,
"Will you marry me?"

— *Ilka Chase*

A man should kiss his wife's
navel every day.

— *Nell Kimball*

I never wanted to weigh more
heavily on a man than
a bird.

— *Coco Chanel*

I am a marvelous housekeeper.
Every time I leave a man,
I keep his house.

— *Zsa Zsa Gabor*

The reason that husbands and
wives do not understand
each other is because they belong
to different sexes.

— *Dorothy Dix*
(Elizabeth Merriwether Gilman)

$\mathcal{S}$ummer bachelors, like summer
breezes, are never as cool as
they pretend to be.

— *Nora Ephron*

*E*ventually he asked her to marry him. In this he showed sense; it is best to marry for purely selfish reasons.

— *Anita Brookner*

$\mathcal{G}$f there is to be any romance in marriage woman must be given every chance to earn a decent living at other occupations. Otherwise no man can be sure that he is loved for himself alone, and that his wife did not come to the Registry Office because she had no luck at the Labor Exchange.

— *Rebecca West*

Of you want to sacrifice the admiration of many men for the criticism of one, go ahead, get married.

— *Katharine Houghton Hepburn*

$\mathcal{T}$he faults of husbands are often caused by the excess virtues of their wives.

— *Colette*

$\mathcal{A}$n archaeologist is the best husband any woman can have: the older she gets, the more interested he is in her.

— *Agatha Christie*

$\mathcal{M}$en who have a pierced ear
are better prepared for
marriage—they've experienced
pain and bought jewelry.

— *Rita Rudner*

I don't hate men, I just wish they'd try harder. They all want to be heroes and all we want is for them to stay at home and help with the housework and the kids. That's not the kind of heroism they enjoy.

— *Jeanette Winterson*

A husband is what is left of a lover, after the nerve has been extracted.

— *Helen Rowland*

*L*ady, Lady, should you meet

One whose ways are all discreet,

One who murmurs that his wife

Is the lodestar of his life,

One who keeps assuring you

That he never was untrue,

Never loved another one . . .

Lady, lady, better run!

— *Dorothy Parker*

*T*here are plenty of men who philander during the summer, to be sure, but they are usually the same lot who philander during the winter—albeit with less convenience.

— *Nora Ephron*

$\mathcal{W}$oman wants monogamy;

Man delights in novelty.

— *Dorothy Parker*

A bachelor is one who travels
alone, without lover or
friend,

But hurries from nothing,
to nought at the end.

— *Ella W. Wilcox*

$\mathcal{T}$he follies which a man regrets
most are those which he
didn't commit when he had the
opportunity.

— *Helen Rowland*

A man in love is incomplete until he is married. Then he's finished.

— *Zsa Zsa Gabor*

$\mathcal{M}$y boyfriend and I broke up. He wanted to get married, and I didn't want him to.

— *Rita Rudner*

*T*he hardest task in a girl's life is
to prove to a man that his
intentions are serious.

— *Helen Rowland*

*I*t has been said that marriage diminishes man, which is often true; but almost always it annihilates woman.

— *Simone de Beauvoir*

$\mathcal{N}$ever marry a man who hates his mother because he'll end up hating you.

— *Jill Bennett*

$\mathcal{W}$henever I date a guy, I think,
is this the man I want my
children to spend their weekends with?

— *Rita Rudner*

Some widowers are bereaved;
others, relieved.

— *Helen Rowland*

*P*eople who are so dreadfully
devoted to their wives are
also apt, from mere habit, to get devoted
to other people's wives as well.

— *Jane Welsh Carlyle*

I don't sit around thinking that I'd like to have another husband; only another man would make me think that way.

— *Lauren Bacall*

*B*efore marriage, a man declares that he would lay down his life to serve you; after marriage, he won't even lay down his newspaper to talk to you.

— *Helen Rowland*

$\mathscr{I}$'ve been married to one Marxist and one Fascist, and neither one would take the garbage out.

— *Lee Grant*

*H*usbands are like fires. They go
out when unattended.

— *Zsa Zsa Gabor*

*H*ome to the man first means mother, as it does to all creatures, but later, and with renewed intensity, it means his own private harem — be it never so monogamous — the secret place where he keeps his most precious possession.

— *Charlotte Perkins Gilman*

A bachelor is one who thinks he is a thing of beauty and a boy forever.

— *Helen Rowland*

*M*arrying a man is like buying something you've been admiring for a long time in a shop window. You may love it when you get it home, but it doesn't always go with everything else.

— *Jean Kerr*

It isn't pathetic anymore to be single. As a friend of mine had the wit to reply when someone asked if she were married, "Good God, no, are *you*?" As much as anything, an unmarried person nowadays is the object of envy.

— *Jane Howard*

$\mathscr{I}$ don't believe man is woman's natural enemy. Perhaps his lawyer is.

— *Shana Alexander*

There is so little difference between
husbands you might as well
keep the first.

— *Adela Rogers St. Johns*

$\mathcal{I}$n our family we don't divorce our men—we bury them.

— *Ruth Gordon*

$\mathcal{W}$hen he is late for dinner and I
know he must be either
having an affair or lying dead in the
street, I always hope he's dead.

— *Judith Viorst*

Family

$\mathcal{I}$ wanted him to cherish and approve of me, not as he had when I was a child, but as the woman I was, who had her own mind and had made her own choices.

— *Adrienne Rich*

*I*t doesn't matter who my father was; it matters who I *remember* he was.

— *Anne Sexton*

*O*ld as she was, she still missed her
daddy sometimes.

— *Gloria Naylor*

$\mathcal{N}$o music is so pleasant to my ears
as that word—father.

— *Lydia Maria Child*

$\mathcal{A}$ king, realizing his incompetence, can either delegate or abdicate his duties. A father can do neither. If only sons could see the paradox, they would understand the dilemma.

— *Marlene Dietrich*

*I*t's only when you grow up, and step back from him, or leave him for your own career and your own home—it's only then that you can measure his greatness and fully appreciate it. Pride reinforces love.

— *Margaret Truman*

$\mathcal{M}$y father died
many years ago,
and yet when something special
happens to me,
I talk to him secretly
not really knowing
whether he hears,
but it makes me feel better
to half believe it.

— *Natasha Josefowitz*

*T*he tie is stronger than that between father and son and father and daughter. . . . The bond is also more complex than the one between mother and daughter. For a woman, a son offers the best chance to know the mysterious male existence.

— *Carole Klein*

The guy's no good—he never was any good . . . his mother should have thrown *him* away and kept the stork.

— *Mae West*

$\mathcal{H}$e is a teenager, after all—a strange agent with holes in his jeans, studs in his ear, a tail down his neck, a cap on his head (backward).

— *Ellen Karsh*

*W*hen a man talks to you about his mother's cooking, pay no attention, for between the ages of 12 and 21, a boy can eat large quantities of anything and never feel it.

— *Sarah Tyson Rorer*

I have nothing to say against uncles in general. They are usually very excellent people, and very convenient to little boys and girls.

— *Dinah Mulock Craik*

*O*nly solitary men know the full joys of friendship. Others have their family, but to a solitary and an exile his friends are everything.

— *Willa Cather*

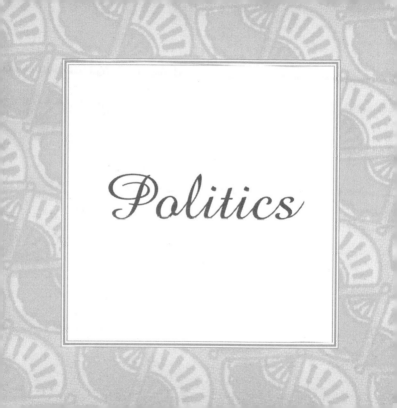

Politics

$\mathcal{H}$e was so crooked, you could
have used his spine for a
safety pin.

— *Dorothy L. Sayers*

$\mathcal{I}$ am working for the time when unqualified blacks, browns, and women join the unqualified men in running our government.

— *Cissy Farenthold*

$\mathcal{A}$ politician is a fellow who will lay down your life for his country.

— *Texas Guinan*

A politician ought to be born a foundling and remain a bachelor.

— *Lady Bird Johnson*

One of the things that politics has taught me is that men are not a reasoned or reasonable sex.

— *Margaret Thatcher*

$\mathcal{I}$t's useless to hold a person to anything he says while he's in love, drunk, or running for office.

— *Shirley MacLaine*

*T*he reason there are so few female
politicians is that it is too much
trouble to put makeup on two faces.

— *Maureen Murphy*

There are far too many men in
politics and not enough
elsewhere.

— *Hermione Gingold*

They say women talk too much. If you have worked in Congress you know that the filibuster was invented by men.

— *Clare Booth Luce*

$\mathcal{O}$n politics, if you want anything said, ask a man; if you want anything done, ask a woman.

— *Margaret Thatcher*

The Double Standard

A man can brave opinion; a woman must submit to it.

— *Madame de Staël*

$\mathcal{W}$omen have to be twice as good to get half as far as men.

— *Agnes MacPhail*

I didn't want to be a boy, ever, but I was outraged that his height and intelligence were graces for him and gaucheries for me.

— *Jane Rule*

$\mathcal{W}$hen a man gives his opinion he's a man. When a woman gives her opinion she's a bitch.

— *Bette Davis*

Once in a Cabinet we had to deal with the fact that there had been an outbreak of assaults on women at night. One minister suggested a curfew: women should stay home after dark. I said, "But it's the men who are attacking the women. If there's to be a curfew, let the men stay home, not the women."

— *Golda Meir*

When men talk about defense,
they always claim to be
protecting women and children,
but they never ask the women and
children what they think.

— *Pat Schroeder*

There is no female Mozart because
  there is no female Jack the
          Ripper.

— *Camille Paglia*

A man has every season while a
woman only has the right to
spring.

— *Jane Fonda*

*W*hatever women do they must do twice as well as men to be thought half as good. Luckily, this is not difficult.

— *Charlotte Whitton*

*O*f reproduction were the chief and only fact of human life, would all men today suffer from "uterus envy"?

— *Betty Friedan*

$\mathcal{W}$hy is it that men can be
bastards and women
must wear pearls and smile?

— *Lynn Hecht Schafren*

$\mathcal{M}$en are taught to apologize
for their weaknesses,
women for their strengths.

— *Lois Wyse*

$\mathcal{A}$ man has to be Joe McCarthy
to be called ruthless.
All a woman has to do is put
you on hold.

— *Marlo Thomas*

*W*hen a man gets up to speak,
people listen, then look.
When a woman gets up, people *look*;
then, if they like what they see,
they listen.

— *Pauline Frederick*

$\mathcal{I}$ earn and pay my own way as a
great many women do today.
Why should unmarried women be
discriminated against—unmarried men
are not.

— *Dinah Shore*

$\mathcal{I}$f there is no word for shrew or slut in male form, is it because there were no bad-tempered, no slovenly men? Or is it because only the male tongue might safely point out defects?

— *Elizabeth Robbins*

*L*egislation and case law still exist in some parts of the United States permitting the "passion shooting" by a husband of a wife; the reverse, of course, is known as homicide.

— *Diane B. Schulder*

Choices

*M*en might feel differently if, before they could have a vasectomy, they had to get a good stern lecture and wait forty-eight hours and get the consent of everybody they know.

— *Louise Slaughter*

$\mathcal{I}$f men could get pregnant, abortion would be a sacrament.

— *Florynce Kennedy*

$\mathscr{D}$id anyone ever tell Toscanini, or
Bach, that he had to choose
between music and family, between art
and a normal life?

— *Elisabeth Mann Borgese*

Feminism

$\mathcal{Y}$ou [men] are not our protectors
. . . If you were, who would
there be to protect us from?

— *Mary Edwards Walker*

I learned that women were smart and capable, could live in community together without men, and in fact did not need men much.

— *Anna Quindlen*

$\mathcal{W}$e are the women that men have
warned us about.

— *Robin Morgan*

$\mathcal{Y}$ou don't have to be anti-man to
be pro-woman.

— *Jane Galvin Lewis*

$\mathcal{I}$t seems to me highly improbable
that women are going to realize their
human potential without alienating
men — some men, anyway.

— *Elizabeth Janeway*

I don't have buried anger against men. Because my anger is right on the surface.

— *Camille Paglia*

*M*en who are physically and
mentally strong are but rarely anti-
feminists.

— *Hannah Mitchell*

The most sympathetic of men never
fully comprehend woman's
concrete situation.

— *Simone de Beauvoir*

A woman without a man is like a
fish without a bicycle.

— *Gloria Steinem*

*W*omen fail to understand how much men hate them.

— *Germaine Greer*

$\mathcal{W}$omen are afraid in a world in which almost half the population bears the guise of the predator, in which no factor—age, dress, or color—distinguishes a man who will harm a woman from one who will not.

— *Marilyn French*

*M*an is preceded by forest,
followed by desert.

— *Anonymous graffiti*

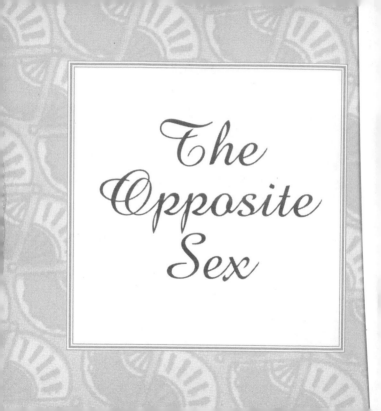

The Opposite Sex

A painting is like a man. If you can live without it, then there isn't much point in having it.

— *Lila Acheson Wallace*

$\mathcal{M}$en were made for war. Without it they wandered greyly about, getting under the feet of the women, who were trying to organize the really important things of life.

— *Alice Thomas Ellis*

*T*he tragedy of machismo is that a man is never quite man enough.

— *Germaine Greer*

$\mathcal{M}$ountains appear more lofty, the nearer they are approached, but great men resemble them not in this particular.

— *Lady Blessington*

$\mathcal{M}$acho doesn't prove mucho.

— *Zsa Zsa Gabor*

*W*hen you've Adam, doesn't it
make you Eve?

— *Anonymous graffiti*

*J*esus was a typical man—they always say they'll come back but you never see them again.

— *Anonymous graffiti*

Three wise men—are you serious?

— *Anonymous graffiti*

*W*hen God created man, she was only experimenting. I always thought men were a phallusy.

— *Anonymous graffiti*

$\mathcal{A}$s for an authentic villain, the real thing, the absolute, the artist, one rarely meets him even once in a lifetime. The ordinary bad hat is always in part a decent fellow.

— *Colette*

*M*en are very confident people. My husband is so confident that when he watches sports on television, he thinks that if he concentrates he can help his team. If the team is in trouble, he coaches the players from our living room, and if they're really in trouble, I have to get off the phone in case they call him.

— *Rita Rudner*

A man hasn't got a corner on
virtue just because his
shoes are shined.

— *Anne Petry*

*W*hat's with you men? Would hair stop growing on your chest if you asked directions somewhere?

— *Erma Bombeck*

*H*e had the uneasy manner of a man who is not among his own kind, and who has not seen enough of the world to feel that all people are in some sense his own kind.

— *Willa Cather*

In all men is evil sleeping; the good man is he who will not awaken it, in himself or in other men.

— *Mary Renault*

When man, Apollo man, rockets into space, it isn't in order to find his brother, I'm quite sure of that. It's to confirm that he *hasn't* any brothers.

— *Françoise Sagan*

*M*an has never been the same
since God died.

He has taken it very hard. Why, you'd
think it was only yesterday,

The way he takes it.

Not that he says much, but he laughs
much louder than he used to,

And he can't bear to be left alone even
for a minute, and he can't

Sit still.

— *Edna St. Vincent Millay*

$\mathcal{M}$en have an easier time buying bathing suits. Women have two types: depressing and more depressing. Men have two types: nerdy and not nerdy.

— *Rita Rudner*

*E*very man I meet wants to protect
me. I can't figure out what from.

— *Mae West*

*T*here is, of course, no reason for the existence of the male sex except that one sometimes needs help with moving the piano.

— *Rebecca West*

*T*he best index to a person's character is a) how he treats people who can't do him any good, and b) how he treats people who can't fight back.

— *Abigail Van Buren*

When a woman behaves like a
man, why doesn't she
behave like a nice man?

— *Edith Evans*

*H*e was about as useful in a crisis
as a sheep.

— *Dorothy Eden*

A male gynecologist is like an
auto mechanic who has
never owned a car.

— *Carrie Snow*

*D*on't accept rides from strange men — and remember that all men are as strange as hell.

— *Robin Morgan*

*I*n men this blunder [chauvinism]
            still you find,

All think their little set mankind.

— *Hannah More*

$\mathcal{I}$f a man says, "I'll call you," and he doesn't, he didn't forget . . . he didn't lose your number . . . he didn't die. He just didn't want to call you.

— *Rita Rudner*

$\mathcal{A}$ man's home may seem to be his castle on the outside; inside, it is more often his nursery.

— *Clare Booth Luce*

There are only two kinds of men —
the dead and the deadly.

— *Helen Rowland*

The cocks may crow, but it's the
hen that lays the egg.

— *Margaret Thatcher*

$\mathcal{M}$en define intelligence, men define usefulness, men tell us what is beautiful, men even tell us what is womanly.

— *Sally Kempton*

*C*hristianity really is a man's religion: there's not much in it for women except docility, obedience, who-sweeps-a-room-as-for-thy-cause, downcast eyes, and death in childbirth. For the men it's better: all power and money and fine robes, the burning of heretics—fun, fun, fun!— and the Inquisition fulminating from the pulpit.

— *Fay Weldon*

The only time a woman really succeeds in changing a man is when he is a baby.

— *Natalie Wood*

$\mathcal{W}$hen I found out I thought God
was white, and a man,
I lost interest.

— *Alice Walker*

$\mathcal{M}$en like war: they do not hold much sway over birth, so they make up for it with death. Unlike women, men menstruate by shedding other people's blood.

— *Lucy Ellman*

$\mathcal{S}$how me a woman who doesn't feel
guilty and I'll show you a man.

— *Erica Jong*

$\mathcal{I}$ can eat a man, but I'm not sure of the fiber content.

— *Jenny Eclair*

*A*ll men are rapists and that's all
they are. They rape us with
their eyes, their laws, and their codes.

— *Marilyn French*

*T*he male is a domestic animal
which, if treated with
firmness and kindness, can be trained
to do most things.

— *Jilly Cooper*

*H*ow can the spirit of the earth
like the white man? . . .
Everywhere the white man has
touched it, it is sore.

— *Wenta Woman*

The reason some men fear older women is they fear their own mortality.

— *Frances Lear*

It is not in giving life but in risking life that man is raised above the animal; that is why superiority has been accorded in humanity not to the sex that brings forth but to that which kills.

— *Simone de Beauvoir*

*M*y ancestors wandered lost in
the wilderness for forty
years because even in biblical times, men
would not stop to ask for directions.

— *Elayne Boosler*

$\mathcal{M}$en are no more immune from emotions than women; we think women are more emotional because the culture lets them give free vent to certain feelings, "feminine" ones, that is, no anger please, but it's okay to turn on the waterworks.

— *Una Stannard*

$\mathcal{A}$ll men are afraid of eyelash curlers. I sleep with one under my pillow, instead of a gun.

— *Rita Rudner*

The art of being a woman can never consist of being a bad imitation of a man.

— *Olga Knopf*

$\mathcal{W}$hy are the needle and the pen

Thought incompatible by men?

— *Esther Lewis*

he trouble about man is twofold.
He cannot learn truths which
are too complicated; he forgets truths
which are too simple.

— *Rebecca West*

$\mathcal{N}$o man is charming all of the time. Even Cary Grant is on record saying he wished he could be Cary Grant.

— *Rita Rudner*

$\mathcal{I}$magine how often women who think they are displaying a positive quality—connecting—are misjudged by men who perceive them as revealing a lack of independence, which the men regard as synonymous with incompetence and insecurity.

— *Deborah Tannen*

$\mathcal{T}$he quietly pacifist peaceful always
die to make room for men
who shout.

— *Alice Walker*

$\mathcal{I}$t's a man's world, and you men
can have it.

— *Katherine Anne Porter*

$\mathcal{M}$en who flatter women do not know them; men who abuse them know them still less.

— *Madame de Salm*

$\mathcal{I}$ wonder why men can get serious at all. They have this delicate long thing hanging outside their bodies, which goes up and down by its own will. If I were a man I would always be laughing at myself.

— *Yoko Ono*

*M*en fear women's strength.

— *Anaïs Nin*

*I*f a woman gets nervous, she'll eat or go shopping. A man will attack a country—it's a whole other way of thinking.

— *Elayne Boosler*

*M*ost women set out to try to change a man, and when they have changed him they do not like him.

— *Marlene Dietrich*

$\mathcal{M}$en cook more, and we all know
why. It is the only interesting
household task. Getting down and
scrubbing the floor is done by women,
or by the women they've hired.

— *Nora Ephron*

$\mathcal{W}$omen who aspire to be as good
as men lack ambition.

— *Anonymous graffiti*

*B*lessed is the man who, having
nothing to say, abstains from
giving in words evidence of the fact.

— *George Eliot (Mary Ann Evans)*

$\mathcal{I}$ fear nothing so much as a man
who is witty all day long.

— *Madame de Sevigné*

Women have got to make the
world safe for men since
men have made it so darned unsafe
for women.

— *Nancy Astor*

*M*en hate to lose. I once beat my husband at tennis. I asked him, "Are we going to have sex again?" He said, "Yes, but not with each other."

— *Rita Rudner*

Women are as old as they feel —
and men are old when they
lose their feelings.

— *Mae West*

$\mathcal{M}$en weren't really the enemy—
they were fellow victims
suffering from an outmoded masculine
mystique that made them feel
unnecessarily inadequate when there
were no bears to kill.

— *Betty Friedan*

Women take clothing much more seriously than men. I've never seen a man walk into a party and say "Oh, my God, I'm so embarrassed; get me out of here. There's another man wearing a black tuxedo."

— *Rita Rudner*

*I*f it's natural to kill why do men have to go into training to learn how?

— *Joan Baez*

$\mathcal{W}$oman's virtue is man's greatest invention.

— *Cornelia Otis Skinner*

*B*eware of men who cry. It's true that men who cry are sensitive to and in touch with feelings, but the only feelings they tend to be sensitive to and in touch with are their own.

— *Nora Ephron*

$\mathcal{W}$omen speak because they wish to speak, whereas a man speaks only when driven to speech by something outside himself—like, for instance, he can't find any clean socks.

— *Jean Kerr*

$\mathscr{I}$t was a pity he couldna be hatched o'er again, an' hatched different.

— *George Eliot (Mary Ann Evans)*

*A*merican women like quiet men:
they think they're listening.

— *Anonymous*

$\mathcal{M}$an forgives woman anything
save the wit to outwit him.

— *Minna Antrim*

I often want to cry. That is the only advantage women have over men — at least they can cry.

— *Jean Rhys*

*F*ighting is essentially a masculine
idea; a woman's weapon is
her tongue.

— *Hermione Gingold*

$\mathcal{M}$en's men: gentle or simple,
they're much of a
muchness.

— *George Eliot (Mary Ann Evans)*

*T*hroughout history females have
picked providers. Males have
picked anything.

— *Margaret Mead*

$\mathcal{I}$'m furious about the women's liberationists. They keep getting up on soapboxes and proclaiming that women are brighter than men. That's true, but it should be kept very quiet or it ruins the whole racket.

— *Anita Loos*

(Self)
Esteem

$\mathcal{H}$e who despises himself esteems
himself as a self-despiser.

— *Susan Sontag*

$\mathcal{M}$en look *at* themselves in mirrors. Women look *for* themselves.

— *Elissa Melamed*

The types who make passes at girls who wear glasses — so they can see themselves in the reflection.

— *Stephanie Calman*

I don't need a man to rectify my existence. The most profound relationship we'll ever have is the one with ourselves.

— *Shirley MacLaine*

When someone sings his own
praises, he always gets the
tune too high.

— *Mary H. Waldrip*

$\mathcal{L}$et's face it, when an attractive but aloof man comes along, there are some of us who offer to shine his shoes with our underpants.

— *Lynda Barry*

$\mathcal{H}$e was like a cock who thought
the sun had risen to hear
him crow.

— *George Eliot (Mary Ann Evans)*

$\mathcal{M}$en are monopolists

of "stars, garters, buttons

and other shining baubles"—

unfit to be the guardians

of another person's happiness.

— *Marianne Moore*

$\mathcal{W}$omen have served all these
centuries as looking-
glasses possessing the magic and
delicious power of reflecting the figure
of man at twice its natural size.

— *Virginia Woolf*

I am a woman meant for a man, but I never found a man who could compete.

— *Bette Davis*

$\mathcal{T}$he vanity of man revolts from the
serene indifference of the cat.

— *Joan Robinson*

$\mathcal{M}$en are irrelevant. Women are happy or unhappy, fulfilled or unfulfilled, and it has nothing to do with men.

— *Fay Weldon*